T0130450

God's Love
doesn't depend on things that we do

DAN HALFMAN

Copyright © 2021 Dan Halfman.

All rights reserved. No part of this book may be used or reproduced by any means, graphic, electronic, or mechanical, including photocopying, recording, taping or by any information storage retrieval system without the written permission of the author except in the case of brief quotations embodied in critical articles and reviews.

WestBow Press
A Division of Thomas Nelson & Zondervan
1663 Liberty Drive
Bloomington, IN 47403
www.westbowpress.com
844-714-3454

Because of the dynamic nature of the Internet, any web addresses or links contained in this book may have changed since publication and may no longer be valid. The views expressed in this work are solely those of the author and do not necessarily reflect the views of the publisher, and the publisher hereby disclaims any responsibility for them.

Scripture quotations are from the ESV® Bible (The Holy Bible, English Standard Version®), copyright © 2001 by Crossway, a publishing ministry of Good News Publishers. Used by permission. All rights reserved.

ISBN: 978-1-6642-3644-8 (sc)
ISBN: 978-1-6642-3646-2 (hc)
ISBN: 978-1-6642-3645-5 (e)

Library of Congress Control Number: 2021911258

WestBow Press rev. date: 08/09/2021

WESTBOW
PRESS®
A DIVISION OF THOMAS NELSON
& ZONDERVAN

— For the Gospel

— For my wife, who shows me God's love every day by loving me no matter what

I know God loves me; Jesus does too.
But sometimes I wonder: Will
this always be true?

When I am good, well,
that makes sense.
God is happy; no one is tense.

But what if I'm bad? What if I mess up?
If I don't deserve it, does that love just stop?

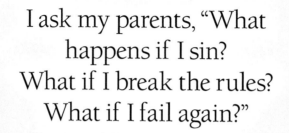

I ask my parents, "What happens if I sin? What if I break the rules? What if I fail again?"

Our word "sin" originally comes from the Greek word hamartanó, which means "to miss the mark" or "to do wrong". This was actually an archery term used when the archer missed the center. We all "miss the mark" when we fall short of God's perfect standard. "For all have sinned and fall short of the glory of God." (Romans 3:23 ESV)

WHAT IF I MAKE A MESS?

GOD LOVES YOU!

WHAT IF I BREAK SOMETHING?

GOD LOVES YOU!

WHAT IF I PUSH MY SISTER?

GOD LOVES YOU!

WHAT IF I BITE MY FRIEND?

GOD LOVES YOU!

WHAT IF WE GET INTO A FIGHT?

GOD LOVES YOU!

WHAT IF I DON'T LISTEN?

GOD LOVES YOU!

WHAT IF I DON'T FINISH MY DINNER?

GOD LOVES YOU!

WHAT IF I GET ANGRY?

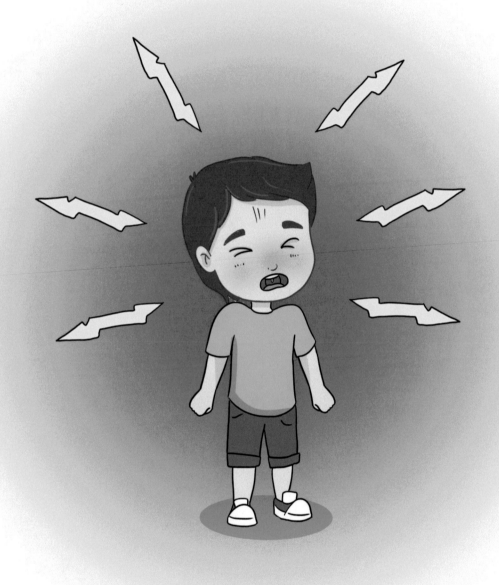

GOD LOVES YOU!

WHAT IF I DONT MAKE THE TEAM?

GOD LOVES YOU!

WHAT IF I FAIL MY TEST?

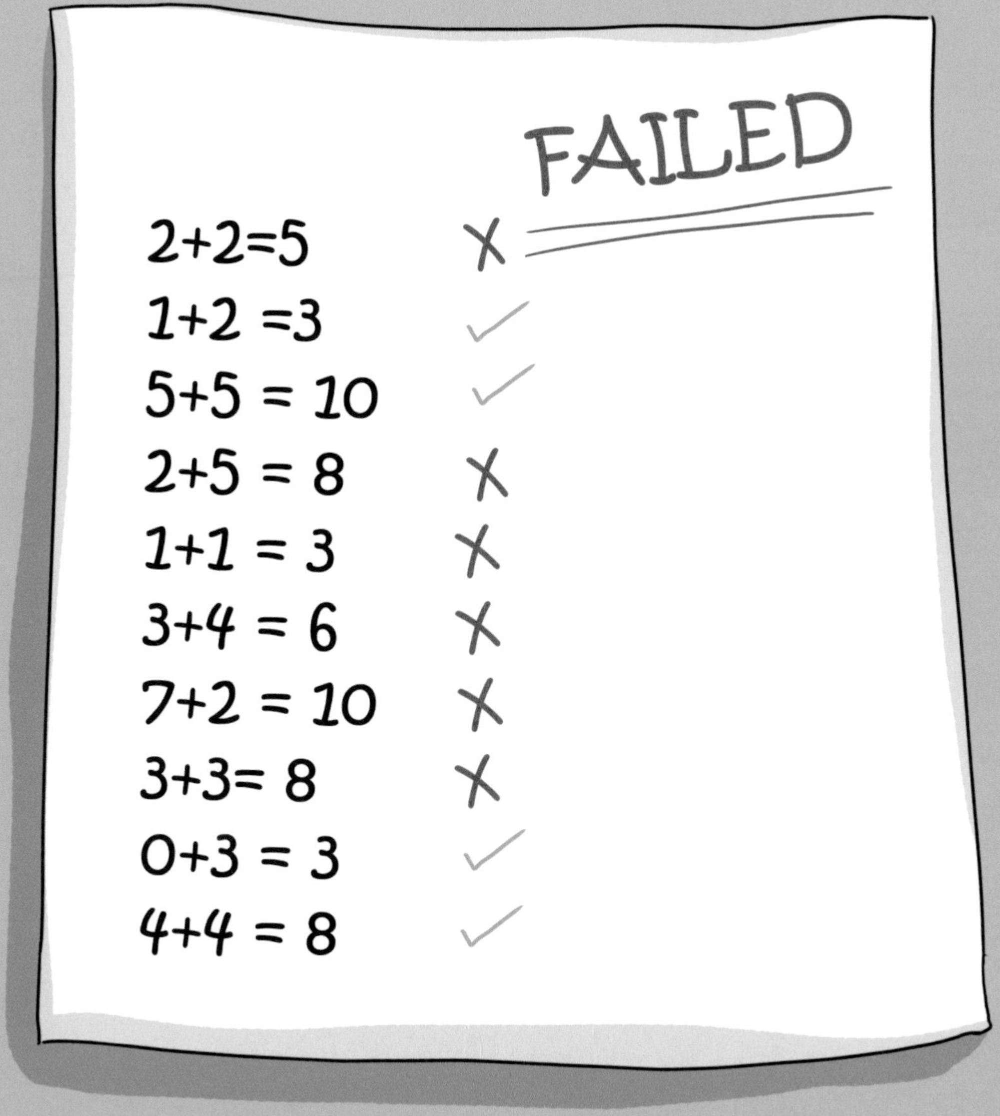

FAILED

2+2=5 ✗

1+2 =3 ✓

5+5 = 10 ✓

2+5 = 8 ✗

1+1 = 3 ✗

3+4 = 6 ✗

7+2 = 10 ✗

3+3= 8 ✗

0+3 = 3 ✓

4+4 = 8 ✓

GOD LOVES YOU!

WHAT IF I DONT DESERVE TO BE LOVED?

GOD LOVES YOU!

I think those are all my questions, at least all I can think of. It looks like there's nothing I can do to fall out of God's love.

Romans 8:38-39 ESV

For I am sure that neither death nor life, nor angels nor ...ers, nor things ...nor things ...owers, nor depth, nor anything else in all creation, will be able to separate us from the love of God in Christ Jesus our Lord."

My parents clearly explain that we *all* sin.
We all mess up, again and again.
God knows we're not perfect; he sees all of our flaws.
He knows we fall short and break most of his laws.

1 - You shall not worship any other gods

2- You shall not worship idols

3- You shall not use the Lord's name in vain

4- You shall remember the sabbath day

5- You shall honor your father and mother

6- You shall not murder

7- You shall not commit adultery

8 - You shall not steal

9 - You shall not lie

10 - You shall not covet

But God loves us so much; he's not done with us yet.
He gave up his Son to pay our whole debt.
We didn't deserve it, and really, still don't.
We didn't *earn* salvation; we can't, and we won't.

They read scripture again; this I know I can trust.
"But God shows his love for us in that while we were
still sinners, Christ died for us." (Romans 5:8 ESV)

They tell me what I have to do;
they show me the key.
What I need to do is simply believe.

Jesus was crucified,
died, and was
buried for *me*.

He rose a few days later, specifically three.

And if I believe this with all my heart, my sins are forgiven; it's like a fresh start.

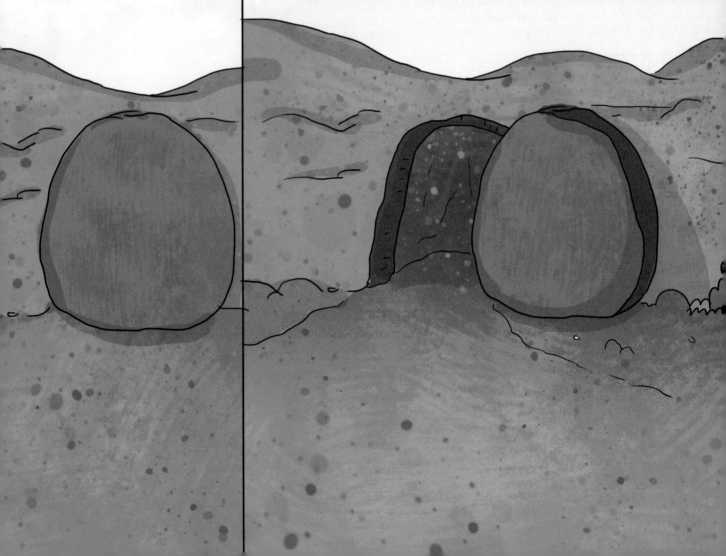

So we don't earn God's love; we
can't deserve more or less—
whether we're good or bad, clean or a mess.
God's love doesn't depend on things that we do.
God will always love me, and
He will always love you!

Ephesians 2:4-9 ESV

But God, being rich in mercy, because of the great love with which he loved us, even when we were dead in our trespasses, made us alive together with Christ— by grace you have been saved— and raised us up with him and seated us with him in the heavenly places in Christ Jesus,

so that in the coming ages he might show the immeasurable riches of his grace in kindness toward us in Christ Jesus. For by grace you have been saved through faith. And this is not your own doing; it is the gift of God, not a result of works, so that no one may boast.

Printed in the United States
by Baker & Taylor Publisher Services